True-To-Life Stories for *Young Teens*

It's My Life

Michael L. Sherer

AUGSBURG Publishing House • Minneapolis

IT'S MY LIFE
True-to-Life Stories for Young Teens

Scripture quotations unless otherwise noted are from the Holy Bible: New International Version. Copyright 1978 by the New York International Bible Society. Used by permission of Zondervan Bible Publishers.

Photos: Barbara Gannon, 12; Jim Whitmer, 24; Dan Stutz, 32; Steve Takatsuno, 42; Will and Angie Rumpf, 52; Gail Int Veldt, 62, 72; Roger W. Neal, 82; Gene Plaisted, 90; Ron Meyer, 100.

Library of Congress Cataloging-in-Publication Data

Sherer, Michael L.
  IT'S MY LIFE.

  (True-to-life stories for young teens)
  Summary: Ten short stories featuring teenagers with decisions to make, living ordinary lives, and trying to do the best they can.
  [1. Conduct of life—Fiction.   2. Short stories]
I. Title.   II. Series.
PZ7.S54476It 1986   [Fic]   86-17448
ISBN 0-8066-2216-4

Manufactured in the U.S.A.   APH 10-3454

1   2   3   4   5   6   7   8   9   0   1   2   3   4   5   6   7   8   9

For Heidi
and her generation

Contents

About This Book

"It's my life—leave me alone!" Is that the way you feel sometimes? It *is* your life. You may have gotten the impression you're the only one who thinks that sometimes. Parents can forget they aren't always going to be around to make decisions for us. In fact, before too long they won't have much to say at all about the choices we must make.

The same is true for teachers and the other people in our lives who seem to want to help control what we decide to do. Before too long they'll have to let us make our own decisions. Perhaps that's why they seem to keep the reins on us when we are trying to discover who we are. It just may be they know how quickly it will come—that day when they must leave off giving their advice.

It can be sort of scary when you think about it: if it really *is* your life (and, honestly, it is), that means you can do almost anything you want to with it. Have you ever wondered where you'd end up after doing exactly what you felt like doing without worrying how it might affect the people you do it to or with? John Southmoor finally asked himself that question in the first story in this book. Or have you ever wondered what would happen if you got the chance to share the glory with an older brother, just like Skeeter Simpson did? Check out the second story to find out.

The 10 short stories in this book are about kids who are a lot like you. They have their lives to live. They realize they can use all the help they can get. But they know, too, that sooner or later it's up to them to make their mark and find their own way to the future.

If this book helps you to figure out a little more about exactly who you are, then writing it has been worthwhile. If the 10 teenagers who are the main characters in these 10 stories help you to make just a little more sense out of your life right now, then your taking the time to read about them will have been worthwhile too.

Don't forget: a lot of people are rooting for you, hoping you can figure out something special to do with your life. Even though you can't escape your family, teachers, classmates, pastor; even though your life is mixed up with a lot of other people's lives; it's still *your life*. With God's help, what can you do with it? Let the people in the stories in this book give you some clues. Then you decide.

Good luck. And happy reading.

One on One

John Southmoor loved basketball more than almost anything. He knew every house in the neighborhood that had a hoop on a pole or above the garage door. If there was a game in progress, he was usually involved.

John had been the star forward on the team at Central Junior High last winter. Now that summer had come, he wanted to be sure to keep his form so that he could try out for varsity at Warren High next year.

That's why he was so excited when the pastor told him on the way out of church one Sunday morning that the city had decided to construct a regulation size court in a new park next door to the church. That would be the closest court to John's house. And, with new asphalt, it would be smoother than the courts he'd had to cycle to down by the Junior High.

John kept his eye on the bare spot where they were going to put the court. Each Sunday, on his way into church, he stole a glance in that direction. And afterwards, while his dad was involved with helping count the offering in the church office, he'd go down the hill and stand and stare at the smooth surface where the bulldozers had cut the ground away.

One Sunday morning he saw the goals in place. He found it difficult to concentrate until the pastor said the benediction. Slipping out the side door of the worship area, he dashed across the church lawn and down to the park. The asphalt was in place! The lines were painted! And the hoops and nets were on the backboards!

After dinner he was on his bike and heading back towards church, a pair of Nikes on his feet, his basketball tucked underneath one arm. Three other boys about his size were there already, shooting baskets, trying to outdo each other. John knew Craig, a tall and lanky friend from church. The other two he wasn't sure he'd seen before.

"Hey, Southmoor!" Craig yelled, seeing him ride up. "Come on down! This court's incredible!"

John parked his bike and walked down to the court.

"Hey, fellas, this is John," Craig said. "John, this is Tom—and 'Stick,' two friends of mine from school."

John sized up Stick and figured he had been well-named.

"Hey, look, let's get a little scrimmage going," Craig suggested. Everybody nodded. All the basketballs were tossed aside except the one Craig held. "What say if Southmoor here and I take on the two of you? OK?" Craig said, as though it had been settled. The other two grinned, nodding their agreement. "Good," Craig said and trotted out of bounds. "We'll take it out."

John had played basketball with Craig at confirmation camp. He knew he was a tough competitor. To be teamed with him, and to be competing on this smooth new court, gave him a feeling of well-being. Tom and Stick were every bit as good. The baskets hardly rested all the while the two teams fought it out. Swoosh! Tom lofted in a long outside shot. Swoosh! Craig hooked one smoothly through the net. Swoosh! Swoosh! The score went back and forth in seesaw fashion for three-quarters of an hour. By that time all four of them were huffing with exhaustion.

"Good game, guys. I gotta go," Stick said when they were tied at 42 apiece.

"Same here," said Tom. John waved them off as they scooped up their basketballs, trudged up the hill, and disappeared. Craig stood at center court and sent a high, smooth-arching shot straight through the hoop.

"You going out for varsity next fall?" John asked.

"You bet your Nikes," Craig said. "Tom and Stick are too. We'll all be in the same school come September. Getting on the team won't be so easy."

"Right," said John, imitating Craig's last shot. The ball whanged noisily against the rim but failed to fall inside.

"With shooting like that, you'll be lucky to get on the team," said Craig. John screwed his face into a frown. "Just kidding," Craig said, tousling John's damp hair. "We really showed those two some fancy shooting, didn't we?"

"Sure did," John said, repeating the long shot he'd missed before. This time it sailed through silently.

"Look, Southmoor, I gotta go. See you."

John watched Craig hike up the hill. He wanted to enjoy this slick new court a little longer. After Craig was gone, he practiced jump shots, lay-ups, free throws, hooks, and shots from the outside. When he was tired but satisfied, he stretched out on the grassy slope beside the court and closed his eyes. His heart was pounding and he heaved to catch his breath. The perspiration tingled on his scalp and neck and arms and chest.

Wha-a-ang!

John opened his eyes and sat up. The rim was vibrating. A girl—about his age, he guessed—had shot and missed. Where had *she* come from? Wha-a-ang! She shot and missed again. Her form was good though. In more ways than one, John noticed. She was slim and pretty, with a cute face and short hair. Her white shorts accented smooth legs. She really was a fox!

Wha-a-ang! Once more she failed to put the ball where she'd intended.

John got up, feeling superior and a little bit benevolent. Perhaps he could give her a clue or two about the finer points of scoring. She was probably not confident enough when she let go each time.

"Hi." John felt his face grow warm as he stepped toward her.

"Hi there," she replied.

"You—want to shoot some baskets?"

"I am already. Thanks."

"Yeah—well—you just missed the last three."

"Right. Just warming up."

John grinned.

"You think that's funny?" she asked, scowling.

"Huh? Oh. No. No, of course not." But he grinned again.

"OK, look, wise guy. If you're such a hotshot, tell you what. Let's try some one-on-one."

"Oh, come on. I wasn't making fun of you or anything. I just meant—"

"That you think I couldn't hit the broad side of a barn. Well, I can handle you. Or are you too embarrassed to go one-on-one with someone who just happens to be female?"

John had never scrimmaged with a girl. Did she have any notion just how good he was? From the looks of things, her shooting wasn't much to brag about. Still, there was nobody around, in case he should humiliate her. And she did have spunk. Besides, she was so dog-goned cute.

"OK. You asked for it. You're on."

"Fine," she replied. "You take it out." She fired the ball into his midsection and almost winded him. It caught John by surprise. He dribbled out of bounds, then stepped back in and started down toward the basket. She watched him like a hawk, then, suddenly, snatched at the ball and stole it easily from him. He whirled and went on the defensive, angry at himself, his face half-flushed with shame. How had she caught him napping like that?

Now she pressed down toward the basket. He gave her room. *No point in pushing her too hard,* he told himself.

She jumped and sent it arching perfectly. He heard it swoosh through almost silently and felt a sourness churning in his stomach. This was going to be a bit more complicated than he'd thought.

Within 20 minutes she was leading him by 14 points. He couldn't stop her jump shots. Where had she become so good at that?

"You want to quit?" she asked, not even sounding winded.

"Huh? Heck no." Now he was getting mad. He drove in for a lay-up. She tried blocking him. He crashed into her, falling to the asphalt half on top of her.

"You hurt?" John asked, feeling foolish and clumsy.

"No, I'm fine. But I think we'd better call it quits for now," she said. "I think you're getting tired."

"Look—"

"Listen, I know you were practicing a long time here before I came. I saw you when I rode by earlier. And before that you were scrimmaging. You ought to be exhausted. I would be."

John grinned at her. "Yeah. Actually, I am." The feeling of her smooth leg next to his sent a tingle through him. Getting up, he offered her his hand.

"How did you get so good?" he asked as they walked over to the grassy slope and sat down to recover for a minute.

"Playing basketball," she answered with a matter-of-fact tone. "I'm varsity at Coolidge Junior High."

"The girls' team," John said. "Man, you've got a wicked jump shot."

"Thanks. Look, you want to try this again? You probably could beat me when you're rested."

"Huh? Oh. Well, OK. Tomorrow afternoon?"

They fought it out a second time the next day. She won again, this time by seven. And then again on Tuesday, by a dozen. "Rats," he said, as they were catching their breath afterwards, "let's face it, I can't beat you."

"Too bad. I really thought you could," she said. He felt like punching her. But she was so good-natured about it, and grinned in such an unself-conscious way, he had to laugh.

"You're really something else," he said. "I kind of like you."

"You're cute when you're exhausted," she said, brushing a strand of his moist hair back against his soggy scalp. He liked the feeling of her doing it.

"I'll tell you what," he said. "Let's do something a little less competitive. You want to bike hike out to Folsom Woods tomorrow afternoon?"

"Sure. Why not? Good for the lungs and legs," she said. "You want to meet here first?"

"Sounds good."

"You know what's kind of crazy about this?"

"What?"

"You don't know my name and I don't know yours either."

When he arrived the next day, Beth was waiting for him, a knapsack hanging from one hand. They cycled, side by side, down to the asphalt bike path, then took off single file, John leading, for the woods. In three-quarters of an hour they were there. They chained the bikes together, securing them to a tree with John's padlock, and hiked a ways into the woods. When they found a secluded spot, they sat down and enjoyed the sounds of birds around them.

"I've been here before," John said. "I don't think anybody ever comes in here."

"Nice," said Beth. "Listen, you want something to eat?"

"Like what?"

"7-Up? Granola Bars?"

"Sure."

They ate in silence. Then John screwed up his confidence and said, "I really like your looks. You're really very pretty."

20

"You're kind of cute yourself, you know."

Before he knew it, he was leaning over, kissing her. To his surprise, she drew her arm around his neck and kissed him back. He felt his body firming and becoming warm. His hand reached over and caressed her arm and breast. She pulled his hand away and drew back from him.

"John, be careful. I think things are getting out of hand." She had a serious look about her.

"There's no one here," John said.

"I know. That's not what's bothering me."

He sat up straight and looked at her. He nudged his empty 7-Up can with his toe. "You ever make love with someone?" he asked.

"No. You?"

"No. But if I did, you'd be the one I'd like to do it with."

"Thanks for the compliment—I guess."

"You guess? What does that mean?"

"A lot of girls my age are having sex with boys. That's not for me. There's just too much at stake."

John knew some of his friends at school had talked about the things they'd done with girls. A couple of them probably had really done it. He had never gone this far himself with any girl before. "There are ways to protect yourself," he said.

"I know," she said. "But there's more to it than not getting pregnant. It—it isn't right. It ought to wait until you're married. That's all."

John had heard that from his parents, from his pastor, and from his Bible class teacher. And a part of him agreed. But something in the eagerness his body felt did not agree at all.

"You understand?" she asked. He nodded, smiling guardedly. "You mad?" He shook his head. He wasn't, really. Actually, he felt a sort of admiration for the way she'd handled it.

"Still friends?" she asked, as they walked back toward the bikes.

"Of course not," he said, scowling in mock aggravation. "I'm still out to trample you at one-on-one. You going to let me have another chance tomorrow?"

"Sure. You're on," she answered, as they pushed off on the path toward home.

"Flee from sexual immorality. All other sins a man commits are outside his body, but he who sins sexually sins against his own body. Do you not know that your body is a temple of the Holy Spirit, who is in you, whom you have received from God? You are not your own; you were bought at a price. Therefore honor God with your body."

1 Corinthians 6:18-20

Whistler's Brother

Splat!

The oily, white ooze spread across Skeeter Simpson's math book. That was just about the last straw! It was bad enough he'd been left out of Concert Band again this year while his brother, Buzz, was playing first chair trumpet, and he'd have to go and listen to him show off at the concert next Friday night. It was even worse that mom had forced him to take time on his way home from school to pick up Buzz's stupid photographs at Carson's Drugstore.

But this was the crowning blow. Now he had bird droppings on his math book. He had half a notion to use Buzz's photo envelope to scrape the droppings off. If Buzz had not been such a glory grabber, this would not have happened.

Overhead a jet plane rumbled, slowed, and gentled down toward the airport not too far away. This was the park—in fact, this was the very picnic table—where Buzz had set up his telephoto lens to shoot those slides of airplanes. Since the park was right below the flight path, it turned out to be a perfect spot.

He wondered if the pictures in this envelope were any good. Buzz really had become an expert with a single lens reflex camera. That was why he'd volunteered to Mr. Lewis that he'd shoot the slides to illustrate the music for the band's spring concert.

Skeeter dragged himself up from the bench and trudged toward home. Sometimes he wished he could have been an only child. That way he wouldn't have to live in Buzz's shadow all the time. Living with an older brother was the pits. Especially since Buzz never seemed to fail at anything.

He banged the screen door as he went into the kitchen.

"Careful, Skeeter!" said his mother, sounding irritated. Skeeter slammed his books onto the counter. "What's got into you this afternoon?"

"I'm sick and tired of doing Buzz's dirty work. He could have gone and got his *own* dumb pictures."

"Now, we've been all through this. You know Buzz has extra band rehearsals every day this week and next. The drugstore would be closed before he got there. Besides, you need the exercise. You spend too much time watching television."

Parents! He'd be better off an orphan some days.

"What's this on your math book? Looks like—"

"Yeah. It is."

"Well, get a paper towel and clean it off."

He wondered if the other mothers in the neighborhood were half as cold-hearted as his was. What did it take to get a little sympathy?

Buzz came home at suppertime. He rambled all through mealtime about how superb the concert music sounded. Skeeter couldn't have cared less. He had to sit

25

and listen to it though, because he knew he couldn't leave the table until they had given thanks.

"Hey, Skeeter," Buzz said as they began to clear the table, "Mr. Lewis needs a slide projectionist. You want to do it?"

Was Buzz feeling sorry for him? "Huh? Oh, I don't know."

"I really wish you would. Come on, why don't you?"

Why should he put himself out to show a bunch of stupid pictures Buzz had taken and that Buzz would get the glory for? "Heck, I don't know, Buzz. I'm not really very interested," he mumbled.

"Oh, come on, Skeeter, why not?"

"I'm just not interested, that's all."

Buzz frowned. "I guess I'm in a jam then."

"Why, Buzz?" asked his mother.

"Well, I sort of promised Mr. Lewis that Skeeter would be able to."

"You what!" Skeeter exploded.

"Well—"

"Really, Buzz," said Mrs. Simpson, "you could have asked your brother first."

"It's just that, well, I didn't want to trust those slides to—well—just anybody."

Skeeter straightened. Was that really it? If so, it made him feel a little better. Flattered, even.

His mother turned to him and said, "Well, since he volunteered you, do you think you'd reconsider, Skeeter? I wouldn't blame you if you didn't say yes, but—"

"Oh, what the heck. OK. What do I have to do?"

"Just come to our two last rehearsals next week so you can learn how to make the pictures and the music blend together. Mr. Lewis will show you exactly what to do. OK?"

"I guess," said Skeeter, shrugging.

"These slides your brother took are really something, Skeeter," Mr. Lewis said.

Skeeter nodded. He wished he had taken them.

"I think we'll save them for the final number. All the house lights will go down, and members of the band will play from memory. That big screen will drop down, back behind the band, and when it stops you start to show the slides. Have you ever operated one of these contraptions?"

"Huh? Yeah. Sure. I've done it lots of times."

"OK. We'll play the piece through once while you just flip through all the slides. Your brother has them in the order that he wants them. Why don't you just try to get a feel for when to change from one slide to the next. I'll let you make the decisions on that. OK?"

"Sure." Suddenly he'd started feeling as though he was an important part of this production. Mr. Lewis went back to the podium. The band calmed down and watched for the director's cue. The music started. Skeeter started showing slides up on the big screen. Click. Wow! What a close-up Buzz had shot! Click. Another one! These really *were* good slides. And they seemed to go just right with the music. Click. Click. Click.

As members of the band were filing out, Mr. Lewis came back over. "That was just right, Skeeter. I think you've got just the right feel for this. Can you come to our last practice tomorrow afternoon?"

"Sure," Skeeter said, feeling more professional than he had ever felt before. "Oh, Mr. Lewis?"

"Yes?"

"What was that piece the band just played?"

"It's an old one. The title is 'The High and the Mighty.' Like it?"

Skeeter nodded. "Yeah. It's kind of cool."

Mr. Lewis went to let the screen back up. Skeeter started putting the projector cover on and winding up the cord. He started whistling softly, then more bravely, the tune to "The High and the Mighty." The empty gymnasium reverberated with the clean sound as he glided from one note up to the next.

The next day after school he got to the gymnasium a little early and began to set up the projector. He'd decided to flip through the slides once more, reminding himself just when to change. He started whistling the tune again.

He came to the last slide as he finished whistling the last measures of the piece. At the instant he stopped whistling, something crazy happened. Members of the band, who had been filing in, and Mr. Lewis, who had now arrived, began to clap. The sound of their applause seemed to fill up the echoey gymnasium.

Skeeter turned deep red.

Mr. Lewis came over and said, "I've never heard such good, clean whistling. Did you know the movie where that music first appeared begins with someone whistling, just like you were doing now?"

"No. No, I didn't. Actually, I didn't notice anybody had come in." He really was embarrassed.

"I'd like to make a deal with you," said Mr. Lewis. "If I would put a microphone right here beside you at the concert, would you whistle for the audience, just like you did right now?"

Skeeter wasn't sure he'd heard him right.

"I'm serious. We'd give you the first stanza. Then the band would come in afterwards. OK?"

His head began to spin. He must have answered that he would, because in no time he was practicing it with the band while thinking frantically about how he could stretch the slides out to be long enough to cover both the whistling and the part the band would play.

That night at supper Buzz would not shut up about how good the whistling at rehearsal had been. Skeeter couldn't tell if Buzz was really sincere, but it sounded like it.

"Well," said Mr. Simpson, "Looks like we'll have *two* stars in this show."

Buzz took Skeeter to the lobby of the auditorium before the audience began arriving. "Look at this," he said, picking up a program. "These were printed just this afternoon." He handed one to Skeeter. On the cover was a drawing of a jet plane taking off. The title of the concert was "Into the Wild Blue Yonder." Inside on the left side were the names of all the pieces on the program: "Up, Up and Away"; "Fly Me to the Moon"; The U.S. Air Force song; and several others. Where had Mr. Lewis gotten music for so many pieces about flying?

At the bottom of the list was the finale: "The High and the Mighty." And there, printed underneath the title, was something that stopped him short. The second line, in print a little smaller than the title, said "With a Whistling Introduction by Our Special Guest Performer— Skeeter Simpson."

"Special Guest Performer"? Holy cow!

By the time the concert started, Skeeter was convinced his whistling muscles would collapse from nervousness or sheer fright. He tried not to think about it. He sat with his folks in the fourth row, on the aisle, where he could get to the projector at the right time.

The concert sounded great. Before he knew it, it was time for the finale. Skeeter slipped out of his chair and stepped up to the microphone at the projector. The house lights dimmed. Suddenly his heart was pounding. He was sure the thumping could be heard through the PA system, all over the gymnasium. He switched the projector on. A beautiful, proud airplane filled the screen. The audience gasped with appreciation.

Without a hint of fear or effort he began to whistle, clean and strong, the melody to "The High and the Mighty" and to change the slides his brother Buzz had taken. Just like clockwork, Mr. Lewis brought the band in at the proper moment. Music filled the room as jet planes soared across the screen.

When it was over he was stunned to hear his name announced from the podium. Mr. Lewis was asking him to come up to the front. He stumbled numbly to the stage.

"I'd like to introduce our fine projectionist," said Mr. Lewis, with his arm on Skeeter's shoulder. "As you know, Skeeter Simpson also did the whistling for our final number."

This time the audience was clapping just for him.

Then Mr. Lewis turned and looked at Buzz. He had him stand. "And it might interest you," he said, looking at the audience, "that Buzz Simpson, our first chair trumpet player, is 'Whistler's Brother.' "

The audience laughed, then broke into applause again.

Their pastor bumped into the Simpsons as they tried to push their way out through the lobby. Buzz had wandered off somewhere to talk to someone in the band. But Skeeter heard the pastor say to his dad, "You've got hidden talent in your family." Looking at Skeeter, he said, "Good work, Skeeter." Then, winking at his dad, he said, "When you see him, give my compliments to 'Whistler's Brother' too."

"To each one of us grace has been given as Christ apportioned it."

Ephesians 4:7

The Other Shoe

Sandy slammed the door so hard it made the windows on the front porch rattle. Had her mother been home at the time, she wouldn't have been able to ignore the sound of it, the way she ignored so many other things that Sandy did these days. But, as usual, her mother wasn't home.

No matter, Sandy told herself, lugging the heavy suitcase down the sidewalk. With her mother gone, it made leaving easier. This way she had been able to pack up her things in peace and quiet and get away without another argument.

Why did they argue so much anyway? Sometimes, when both of them were home, it seemed to be the only thing they did. The fact that her mother worked two jobs didn't help, of course. Having to pay all the bills and raise Sandy without a father around was not easy. Still, she didn't have to be so short-tempered and sarcastic all the time.

Sandy's arm began to ache. She shifted the suitcase to the other side and stepped down the curb. She began to wonder if she could make it the seven blocks to the Fosters before she collapsed. She almost wished some driver she knew would come by so she could hitch a ride. But, on the other hand, this way she wouldn't have to do any explaining about the suitcase.

It would be 9:00 tonight before her mother would be home. Sandy wondered if her mom would figure out that she had gone to Cliff's house. When she discovered what had happened, would she be upset? The way things were between the two of them these days, Sandy doubted it. Maybe her mom would be as glad to have her gone as she felt about leaving.

Three blocks down and four to go. The walk to the Fosters seemed much farther while lugging something heavy. What would Cliff say when she walked in like this? He was expecting her to come over to do homework. Well, her books were in the suitcase. But so was everything else she valued in this world. Well, almost. There was only so much you could stuff into a suitcase.

At last Cliff's house came into view. She shifted the suitcase to the other arm again and trudged the last block with added energy. Cliff's folks were seldom home this time of day. She hoped that was the way things were today. She needed time to talk with Cliff before they tried confronting his parents with anything.

As she reached the porch she felt her confidence begin to slip. Suppose Cliff laughed at her, or scolded her, or wouldn't go along with it? He might just think she was a nitwit or something, leaving home like this and expecting him to take her in. Well, that was a chance she would have to take.

She rang the bell.

Suddenly she felt exposed. The neighbors could be watching her right now, making up wild stories about some girl with a suitcase moving in with Cliff. She wondered why he didn't come to the door. She knew he was at home. When she'd seen him in the school lunchroom earlier today, she'd told him she'd be coming over. So what was taking him so long?

She tried the door. It wasn't locked. She stepped inside and dragged the suitcase with her, standing it beside the bannister.

"Cliff?" Silence. Was he home or wasn't he? "Cliff? You here?" She thought she heard an answer from the basement. She went to the stairwell and opened the basement door. "Cliff?"

She heard the sound of metal banging against metal. "Sandy? Come on down!" He sounded out of breath.

She found him in the exercise room his dad had fixed up in one corner. Cliff's dad had remodeled the basement, making the front just like a small apartment, with a fireplace room, a bathroom, and a bedroom. The back half was the laundry area and the exercise room.

Cliff was lying on his back on the wrestling mat, a heavy set of weights across his chest. He was wearing gym shorts, but no shirt or shoes. The smell of perspiration told her he'd been at it for a while. On him, she sort of liked the smell.

Cliff pushed the bar up from his chest. She watched his arms strain as his muscles bulged. His face was turning red, the vessels standing out along his neck and temples. She held her breath until he had the bar all the way up. He locked his elbows in position, holding the weight above him.

"Sorry I'm not finished here," he said, still staring at the weights. "You're early."

"Yeah," she said. "I know. I just decided to come over sooner."

Cliff eased the weights back to the mat, then rolled them off his chest and sat up. "Good for the arms and shoulders," he said, grinning at her.

"Yeah," she said, sitting down on the edge of the mat. She returned his grin. "You're pretty good at it."

"Not half as good as dad. You ought to see him lift them."

Sandy wasn't interested in Cliff's dad. It was Cliff she cared about. She wondered if he realized exactly how she felt about him. "Are you going to lift some more?"

"No. Let me clean up and change. You bring your books?"

"Yeah." Should she tell him what else she'd brought? "You want to stay for supper afterwards?"

"Supper?" She had better tell him. "Listen, Cliff—"

"Yeah?"

"I just did something that might be kind of stupid."

"What's that?"

"I—just moved out on my mom."

"You *what*?"

"I left my suitcase upstairs in your hall."

Cliff gave out a long, low whistle. "Sandy, you don't want to move in *here*!"

Why did he have to be so negative right off the bat? "Look, Cliff, you know how rotten things are at my place. I just can't take it any more. I had to get out—for a while."

"Look," Cliff said, getting up, "I'd better shower. Then let's talk about it. Why don't you go up and bring your suitcase down here to the guest room."

"Thanks," she said, smiling. Something told her half the battle had been won.

"See you in a couple minutes," Cliff said, heading for the guest room where the shower was.

Sandy went upstairs and grabbed the suitcase. Suddenly it wasn't nearly as heavy as it had been just a little while ago. She eased it down the stairs and set it in the fireplace room. She stretched out on the bed and listened to Cliff washing in the shower. The water stopped. She sat up, staring at the bathroom door. A minute later he came out, a towel around his middle. "You surprised me, coming so early," he said. "My clothes are upstairs in my room."

"That's OK," she teased. "I like your outfit."

Cliff self-consciously snugged up the towel. "Look," he said, fingering the damp hair on his scalp, "I think you could stay here a day or two. But I don't know about much longer than that."

"That's OK," she said appreciatively. Her throat felt thick. She should have known it might not work to walk in unannounced like this and think she could just take up residence. No matter. Two days were two days.

He had said two days, hadn't he?

Cliff's mother had outdone herself again. The dinner was spectacular. It was the third one Sandy had shared with the Fosters since she'd left home. As Mr. Foster brought dessert around, he said, "Our daughter, Sue, will be here in the morning. I think we've got it all worked out now. You can stay with her rent-free and earn your meals by baby-sitting with her two preschoolers. The money that she'll save on day-care will provide enough to buy your groceries. Of course, you'll have to go straight there every day when school is out. Her job begins at 4:00 each afternoon."

"I really do appreciate your making the arrangements," Sandy said, positioning a chunk of ice cream on the piece of cherry pie she was about to devour. "I just need time to think things through. I hope Sue doesn't mind."

"No, not at all, dear," Mrs. Foster said. "I hope you don't mind terribly that I explained it to your mother. I just felt responsible to her. She must have worried, don't you see?"

Sandy nodded. She had been surprised how easily her mom had seemed to go along with Mrs. Foster's explanation. In a way, she even felt a little angry that her mother didn't fight it. Did that mean she really wanted her out of the house?

"Everything was just delicious, Mrs. Foster," Sandy said, devouring the last mouthful of pie. "Can I help with the dishes?"

"Thanks, Sandy. Cliff will appreciate it, too. I know, since he's on dish duty tonight."

Sandy listened to the clock tick. She was bored with television, and Sue's radio was broken. Sandy had done her homework, and she wasn't tired enough to go to bed. She couldn't phone Cliff for a second time; he'd just hung up a half hour ago.

She really missed him; they didn't see each other as much these days. But, with Sue required to work nights and most weekends, Sandy had to stay at the apartment with her kids. Sue had really been terrific about everything. She'd let Sandy help decide what groceries they should buy and help plan menus. Sandy's mom had made her cook but never asked her for advice about the menu.

Sue had had long talks with Sandy in the mornings before it was time to leave for school. It seemed as though breakfast was the only time the two of them saw each other. But it had been time well spent. Sue had explained to her how difficult it was to try to raise a family without a father around. Since her husband had been killed on a high-line accident while working for the electric company, she had had to go to work. She'd told Sandy that things were not so bad just now, but she was apprehensive about trying to be both a mother and a father to her kids when they came into their teenage years.

For Sandy, living here with Sue had helped things to come into focus in a way they never had before. Although Sue seemed to be more open and was a better listener than her mother, Sandy could see many similarities between the two of them. Both were caught in the same trap; both needed all the help that they could get.

Sue had a way of explaining things so that you really sympathized with her. In fact, she had helped Sandy to realize just how her own mom probably felt about attempting to be both a mother and a father. If her mom could only have been half as sensitive and understanding as Sue was!

But, Sandy realized, her mother couldn't help it that her personality was not like Sue's. She just seemed to be more withdrawn and businesslike, that's all. Sometimes Sandy found herself behaving just the way her mother did. In fact, her grandmother was sort of like that too.

The clock chimed 9:15. She wondered what her mom was doing now. She'd be at home tonight. Had she missed Sandy much? She had never phoned. But that was probably because Cliff's mom had told her things might work out better if she didn't.

Sue had told Sandy she could go to church with them this weekend. Sandy hadn't gone the other times Sue had invited her, but this time she wanted to go with them. There was a problem, though. She had one good pair of shoes for church, but, in her rush to leave, she'd only packed one shoe. The other one was lying somewhere in her closet at home. She wondered if her mom had found it, cleaning up her room and things.

Would Sue mind if she went to church in sneakers? It had been so long since Sandy had attended church, she didn't know what people wore any more. She knew one woman who wore blue jeans when she went. So maybe sneakers wouldn't be so bad.

But, just the same, it would be nice to have that other shoe. Perhaps she could stop by the house, say, after school tomorrow, and just pick it up. Maybe if she phoned her mom, she'd leave the door unlocked.

She wondered. Should she call? What if her mom hung up on her? What if she didn't want her stopping by?

Could it have been three weeks since she'd walked out and slammed the door? And in that time she hadn't bothered once to call her mom and ask her how she was!

Possibly her mom had done some thinking too in all this time. Who could say, perhaps she'd even shed some tears over it. Maybe she was missing her by now.

Sandy wondered what to do. If only Sue were home, she'd ask for her advice. But Sue would only tell her it was her decision. Sue was good at making you decide something yourself and then take the responsibility.

She got up and went to the bedroom where the children were asleep. She pulled the covers up around each one, smoothed their hair, and listened to them breathe.

Then, without another thought, she went into the living room, sat down beside the phone, and started dialing.

"Hello—Mom?—It's Sandy—"

"Get rid of all bitterness, rage and anger, brawling and slander, along with every form of malice. Be kind and compassionate to one another, forgiving each other, just as in Christ God forgave you."

Ephesians 4:31-32

I.O.U.s in the Offering Plate

Brrrrrrring-king-king-king-king! The electronic games in the arcade competed noisily with one another. Tom Jordan fired another salvo at the space invaders and felt exhilaration as he massacred another row of them.

With a surge of energy he finished off the enemy. He looked with satisfaction at the final score. Not bad! This was his second highest ever. Fishing in his pocket for another quarter, he discovered he had spent the last one on this game. Was it possible? That meant he'd spent his whole allowance for the week!

Next to him, Phil Parker was just finishing at Pac Man. "Let's go, Phil," Tom said, and he led the way through the crowded maze of players, noise, and flashing lights. When they reached the sidewalk leading from the shopping center they were almost blinded for a minute; it took a while to get used to daylight after having spent an hour inside the dark arcade.

"How much did you spend, Phil?"

"I don't know. A bunch. I must have played 12 games."

43

"My folks don't like me spending so much time in there," Tom said as they biked along toward Phil's house. "Dad says staring at those games may not be good for you. My mom just thinks I'm wasting time and money."

"Yeah. My folks talk that way too. But they grew up without stuff like this. I don't think they've got a clue about how much fun it is."

"It *does* seem like a lot of money, though," Tom said. "I wonder if the owner of that place is getting rich."

"Yeah, probably," Phil answered, as they headed up the driveway to his house. Inside, Phil found the mail his mother had left on the kitchen table. "Hey, look at this. A postcard from my dad. He's on another business trip in California."

Tom looked at the card. It showed a golf course, palm trees, and the ocean. "When's he coming back?"

"Next week sometime, I think. Hey, look at this, Tom. I'll bet you got one of these at your house too." Phil opened a full-color brochure showing lakes and teenagers canoeing.

"Hey! It's from Camp Wilderness," Tom said. "They must have gotten our deposits and the registration forms."

"Can't wait for July 20. That's just seven weeks away. I hope they put us in the same set of bunk beds."

"They will," Tom said. "I wouldn't even go if I was paired with anybody else."

"Me, either," Phil replied.

On Sunday morning Tom was suddenly embarrassed when his mother asked him, on the way to church, "Do you have your offering envelope?"

"Well, I—ran a little short this week," he answered awkwardly.

"Didn't you save 10% when you got your allowance last Monday?"

"I guess I forgot."

His father said, "Suppose I start forgetting to give you allowances?" Tom squirmed. "That *was* what we agreed. Remember?"

"Yeah." Those last two games of Space Invaders had cost him what he should have saved for church. "I'll put in double next week, dad."

"OK," his father said. "But take it out on Monday. Understand?"

"Right." Tom resolved not to get in a jam like this again.

In church the pastor preached about three servants who were given treasure to invest for their employer. It was shorter than the pastor's usual sermons. Afterwards a member of the stewardship committee got up and said, "We are going to pass the offering plates two times today. This first time, please put in your usual offering. Then, the second time, please take from the plate a white envelope. Inside you will find 10 dollars. We want you to take this money and invest it—any way you like. In the middle of November we'll ask you to bring the 10 dollars back, along with any earnings you have gotten with it. It can be a good reminder of how everything we have is loaned to us from God."

Tom thought that was peculiar. Passing money out to people in the pews? He noticed that his father took an envelope when they came by. He wondered whether he should take one too.

After church he stopped the pastor for a minute. "Were those envelopes for kids my age?"

"I guess we didn't make that very clear, did we? Well, we have extras. Why don't you go ask the chairman of the stewardship committee if she'll give you one."

On the way home Tom thought seriously about how to invest the money in his envelope. When he'd walked out of church with it he'd thought it wouldn't be too difficult. But now he wondered, really, how he could find ways to invest it. Six months seemed like a long time—but not very long to make 10 dollars grow.

"Dad, what will you do with your 10?"

"I think I'll put it in the money market. The interest it's paying now is really not too bad."

Tom didn't want to ask his dad to help, but his own bank account was only earning five percent. There must be something better he could do with the money, he thought. He tucked the envelope inside a dresser drawer and didn't think about it for a week or more.

When Tom rolled up the driveway at Phil's house he hardly could believe his eyes. "For Sale. Jones Realty Company," the shiny metal sign said.

I must have the wrong house! he thought, climbing off his bike and going to the door. Phil's mother let him in. She seemed preoccupied with something.

"Hi, Tom," Phil said, when he appeared around the corner of the living room. "Come on down to my room." When they were stretched out on the floor, Phil said, "Remember when I got that postcard from my dad?"

"Yeah?"

"And you asked when he was coming home?"

"Yeah?"

"Well, last week mom found out that he isn't."

"Coming home?"

46

"That's right. They're getting a divorce." Phil's voice was gloomy.

"Oh, no! Phil, what happened?"

"Don't ask me. It's all a big surprise to me. Now we've got to sell the house and move to an apartment."

"Man, that's lousy, Phil. You sure he won't be coming back?"

"I'm positive. It looks like we'll be cutting back on lots of things. Like my allowance. So I can't go with you to the shopping mall arcade, I guess."

Tom scowled. Then something chilling suddenly occurred to him. "You—won't be cutting out Camp Wilderness—will you?"

Phil nodded, saying nothing.

"Phil, you *have* to go! You've sent the registration fee. It's nonrefundable by now!"

"Don't rub it in, man," Phil said, sounding irritated.

Tom looked the sheet of paper over one more time. According to the figures he had jotted down and added up, he could afford to pay the rest of Phil's camp fee by using his allowances for all the weeks between now and the time they'd leave. If, that is, he also threw in that 10 dollars from the envelope they'd given him at church. He didn't know if people on the stewardship committee would approve of what he planned to do with it. But he would pay it back from his allowance after camp was over. And maybe he could still invest it somewhere—for a month or two.

Each Sunday after that Tom held his breath, in case his parents might inquire about his offering envelope. Luckily they never did. They might not have been too impressed to know that he was putting notes inside his envelopes each week that read "I.O.U. 50¢, to be paid sometime before August 31."

He had a hard time talking Phil into accepting the arrangement. Phil's mom had some argument about "not taking charity," but when Tom said he wouldn't go to camp without Phil, she changed her mind.

At last the middle of July arrived. Tom's dad delivered them to camp and promised to return for them at week's end. They had a terrific time, canoeing with two dozen other teenagers in and out among the islands, camping out on islands three nights out of seven, meeting some great counselors, and learning some new songs, some crazy, some religious. Everything was over much too soon.

It took Tom two weeks after camp was over to pay off the I.O.U.s he'd put into the offering plate so many Sundays in a row. There wasn't much of his allowance left as a result. Then the first two weeks in August he used all of it to put the money back into the envelope he'd gotten from the stewardship committee.

As soon as he had the 10 dollars back, he cycled down to put it into his savings account. He wished he knew somebody with a hot tip on how he could double it within a month or two by buying stocks or something. But he didn't know a thing about investing, and nobody that he knew did either.

Just before the Labor Day weekend, Tom got a phone call.

"Tom? It's Phil."

"What's up?"

"Bad news."

"How bad?"

"Terrible. We're moving."

"What? How far?"

"New York. My mom's got friends there. She can get a job there. So we're moving."

"When?"

"Next Wednesday."

Tom could not believe it. Nor could he believe it when he watched the movers carry out Phil's family's furniture and drive away. Nor could he believe that his best friend suddenly was gone.

He had a hard time starting school that fall. It didn't seem the same without Phil. Slowly, though, he started feeling as though he was getting over it.

He found himself avoiding the street where Phil used to live. He'd cycle some other way, even if it meant a longer trip. And, although he visited the arcade at the shopping mall a time or two, he found he didn't have much interest in it any more. The fun seemed to have gone out of it.

On the weekend before they were to take their "treasure" and their earnings back to church, Tom's dad said something that disturbed him. "I've been calculating," he said. "Since the money market doesn't pay as much when you only invest for six months, I'll only have $10.70 to turn in."

Tom's spine tingled. He had only had his money earning interest for three months, not six, and only at a rate of five percent. He tried to figure out the earnings in his head. That would only come to—12½ cents! Not even enough to play one game of Space Invaders! Suddenly he felt embarrassed and ashamed.

The night before the Sunday morning that the money was to be returned, Tom wrote a letter to the stewardship committee. He told them everything—how he had used the money to help get Phil's camp fee paid, and how he'd written I.O.U.'s to cover for his Sunday offerings, and how he hadn't had much time to reinvest the treasure he'd been given once the week at camp was over. He ended with a paragraph apologizing for not doing better, but he explained that at least he'd given back as much as he'd gotten in the first place.

The next day, during worship, Tom had trouble concentrating. But he snapped to attention when he heard the pastor, in his sermon, read once again the Bible story of the owner who gave money to three servants, especially the part about the one who had buried his money in the ground: "The master said to him, 'You wicked and slothful servant. . . .' "

That's all Tom heard. He started feeling panicky. He felt like crawling underneath the pew. He wished he hadn't written that letter to the stewardship committee. And he wished he hadn't taken any money in the first place.

Two weeks later Tom came home from school and found his mother reading a newsletter from the church. "Here, Tom," she said, "you might be interested in this. It's all about that stewardship committee project that you took part in."

Tom felt a shiver down his spine. He took the letter and began to scan the article. His eyes stopped on one paragraph in particular: ". . . and one of our members invested in another human being. He spent his 10 dollars on a week at camp for someone who could not have gone otherwise. Who can tell how that investment may pay off someday? Not everything we spend for God comes back to us in fatter bank accounts. We think this person caught the deeper meaning of what spending for the Lord is all about."

Tom felt his cheeks flush. He felt as though a burden had been taken off his shoulders. Suddenly he thought of Phil and wondered how things were with him. He wondered if it wasn't time to sit down and write him a letter.

He had all kinds of things to tell him.

"Remember this: Whoever sows sparingly will also reap sparingly, and whoever sows generously will also reap generously. Each man should give what he has decided in his heart to give, not reluctantly or under compulsion, for God loves a cheerful giver. And God is able to make all grace abound to you, so that in all things at all times, having all that you need, you will abound in every good work."

2 Corinthians 9:6-8

Herr Matthew Morgenstern

Mary Stone was running out of time—literally. It happened every school year. She would get involved in far too many things. Last year she'd joined so many clubs she hardly had a chance to get her schoolwork done. Plus there was youth group and choir at church and babysitting.

Her parents told her time and time again they thought she'd end up with a nervous breakdown. At one point last spring they'd finally put their foot down and demanded that she drop out of some of her school activities. There'd been a major crisis over that. She just couldn't find a way to cut out anything.

Somehow, though, she had arranged to drop the camera club and track. Then, through the summer, she had plotted carefully her course for fall. She'd made a list of those activities she wanted to participate in most. She vowed she wouldn't overdo it. And for three months she had succeeded.

But now, the first week in December, she feared she'd gotten on that slippery slope again—too many promises to too many people and activities and far too little time to fit them in. Ironically, the thing that threatened to undo her now was an assignment for an ordinary class at school, not a school activity or club at all! The history teacher had explained how necessary it was to appreciate eyewitness recollections of events. He'd asked a member of the class to volunteer to do an interview with someone who had lived in Germany when Hitler had come to power.

Mary had been tempted by the extra credit that she knew she'd get for doing it. Besides, nobody else had volunteered. And Mary always had had difficulty saying no. So, of course, she found herself appointed.

Now she wondered how she'd find a day to do it and how she would ever find a person fitting the requirements of the project. In the midst of everything, she found herself resenting the assignment. She was angry with herself for saying yes and tempted to go back and tell the teacher she just couldn't do it. But she knew she didn't have the nerve to back out now. No, she'd simply have to face the music and get on with it.

She'd have to find someone who'd lived in Germany at least 50 years ago and had been old enough at the time to remember what had taken place there. She had racked her brain to think of where to find someone like that until, finally, it had come to her: the nursing home. They might have someone like that.

Her church choir had gone to the nursing home to sing last Christmas, so she didn't feel exactly like a stranger going there. But she would have to set aside some extra time to go, and time was what she didn't have right now.

She put it off as long as possible. But as the day for the report drew near, she finally gritted her teeth and made up her mind to go to the nursing home and get it over with. Armed with a notebook and a pen, she started out one Wednesday after school. She had rehearsal for church choir that night, so she would have to make this quick.

It took her 20 minutes to get to the nursing home. The woman at the desk seemed glad to see her. "We don't get too many younger people here," she said. Mary hadn't thought she was so "young," but she shrugged the comment off. She told the woman what she needed.

"Oh, let's see," the woman said. "I don't think we have—"

Good grief, thought Mary, *now I've made this trip for nothing. I should have phoned first.*

"Well, actually, we do have one—"

"Which one is that?" asked Mary hopefully.

"Well, I don't know if you would want to try to talk to him. He's just a little senile."

"Senile?"

"Yes. He gets forgetful and confused sometimes."

She wasn't in a mood to be particular. "I'll take him," she said with a hint of impatience. Immediately she realized she was treating the old man, whoever he was, like a piece of merchandise at an auction.

"Well, it's Mr. Morgenstern. He lived in Germany until the war broke out. But Mr. Morgenstern is—well, I want to caution you—he's very old, and rather frail."

"That's fine," said Mary, smiling. "I just need about a half hour of his time. Could I go in and see him now?"

"I'll ask an aide. Just wait here for a moment."

Mary glanced around the lobby. People sat in wheel-chairs, watching television. One old man was sleeping in an easy chair, his mouth wide open. Mary wondered what it would be like to live here. Not too great, she thought.

"Mr. Morgenstern has just awakened from his nap," the woman said when she returned. "Why don't you go down to his room and see if he can spend a little time with you? If not, you could come back another day."

Mary had no intention of coming back another day. This assignment was soon due, and she had other things to do. Down the hall she went and, stopping at the door whose number matched the one she had been given, softly knocked. Nobody answered. She pushed on the door and stepped inside. Mr. Morgenstern was sitting in a chair beside his bed. He had a bathrobe on, beneath which he wore warm pajamas. He looked at her with a puzzled stare.

She wondered what she'd gotten into. But she sat down on the bed, since he was in the only chair available. "Hello there, Mr. Morgenstern."

"*Vas?*"

He was hard of hearing. Great. Just what she needed. She spoke louder. "Mr. Morgenstern, I'm Mary Stone."

"*Ach, ja. Wie Gehts.*"

She felt panic. Didn't he speak English?

"Mr. Morgenstern, I understand you lived in Germany when Hitler came to power."

"*Ach, ja.* Until 1937. Then I come America."

"Why did you leave?"

"Vell, half of me is Jewish. This half," he said, drawing an imaginary line down his middle and pointing to his right side. He began to laugh. Mary grinned. He had a sense of humor.

"What about your other half?"

"*Not* Jewish. That half could have stayed in Deutschland." He began to laugh again.

And they said he was senile! "Mr. Morgenstern, did you see any of the war? Do you remember any of it?"

"*Ach,* young *fraulein,* I saw Kaiser Vilhelm's Var." She enjoyed the way his W's came out like V's.

"You mean, the First World War?"

"*Ach, ja.*"

"How old were you then?"

"Thirty-one. *Ja.*"

Mary tried to do subtraction in her head. That meant that Mr. Morgenstern must be—more than a hundred years old! How sharp his mind was for a man that old! Or, was he senile after all, and only telling her what he had read about in books? "Mr. Morgenstern, do you remember Kaiser Wilhelm?"

"Vell, I never met him personally." He chuckled. "Listen," he said suddenly, "I must quick an errand do. You stay. I be right back again." He got up slowly and shuffled off toward the bathroom. While he was gone, Mary looked about the room. There were very few items here that looked like personal possessions. On the table by the bed she saw an old brown book. She picked it up and looked inside the cover. On the end paper was lettered "Matthew Morgenstern" in fancy German script. The next page indicated that it was a German Bible. She put the book back just as Mr. Morgenstern came in again.

They talked a little longer. Then an aide came and announced that Mr. Morgenstern would have to go to supper. Mary realized that she was due at home as well.

But she still had not asked all of the questions she'd wanted to ask.

"May I come back and see you one more time?" she asked.

"*Ach, ja,*" he said. "I no go anyplace!" he chuckled.

Mary thanked him for his time and slipped out into the hall. The whole way home she wondered if he really was as old as he had said—and whether anybody ever came to see him any more.

On Saturday she went back to the home. She had never even talked to anybody before who was older than a hundred. Unlike her last trip here, this visit was one she was really looking forward to.

But Mr. Morgenstern was asleep. When they woke him, he was so confused he didn't even recognize her.

"Mr. Morgenstern, don't you remember when I talked to you on Wednesday?"

"*Nein.* Nobody ever comes to see me."

She asked him about Hitler and about the kaiser. He returned a lost and misty stare. She hardly could believe it.

Mary probably would not have gone back to the home except that she was still not ready for the class report. She knew she had to try to visit Mr. Morgenstern once more. She didn't really have the time, but Tuesday after school she hurried over to the nursing home again.

It was as though she hadn't ever left his room the first time she had come. He knew her instantly. They chatted all about the war in Europe. Mr. Morgenstern was full of stories. Some of them were funny; some of them were sad; some of them were horrible. But he clearly was enjoying every minute, telling them to her.

When she knew that she had all she needed for a good report, Mary said, "I think I ought to go now, Mr. Morgenstern."

He took hold of her, and she could feel his body trembling. There were tears beginning in his eyes. He said, "You come again, *ja*? Time goes slow here. No one ever comes. You come back sometime. *Ja*?"

Mary felt guilt and anger rising in her. She was trying to cut down on extra things to do. On the other hand, it probably was true; nobody else ever seemed to come to see him. "Well—OK. I'll try."

"*Dat's gut!*" He let his hand slip from her arm.

Mary hurried home to write her history class report.

She came to see him one more time before the Christmas rush began. Then, with members of the church choir, she came back to sing for him the weekend before Christmas. Some of the choir members said they could remember singing in his room the year before. But Mr. Morgenstern said no, he'd never had a group of singers come into his room before.

Mary realized his memory simply wasn't very good sometimes.

She saw him once in January. He was not too good that day. He didn't seem to know her, but she sat and chatted with him anyway. As she went out, an aide told her it really was important to him to have company.

"Does anybody ever come to see him?" Mary asked.

"Just you."

She thought about that all the way home. Why was she the only one who ever went to see him? Were his relatives all gone? Didn't people realize how interesting he was, and how much wisdom he had stored up in his head?

She wished she had more time to visit him. Then it struck her: she was short of time, but Mr. Morgenstern had plenty. Someday she might be in his shoes. Would she end up sitting in a nursing home somewhere, with nobody to come and say hello? She vowed right then and there that she would drop out of some club or other school activity and make more time for Mr. Morgenstern.

But February came and went, and she was busy.

And March.

On Easter Sunday, heading home from church, Mary realized she hadn't been to see Mr. Morgenstern for a long, long time. After dinner she took an Easter lily from the table in the dining room and headed for the nursing home.

The woman at the desk looked at her sadly. "Mr. Morgenstern died 13 days ago."

Something inside of Mary seemed to snap. It was too late. Why had she waited? Why had no one told her that he'd died?

She asked where they had buried him. She knew the cemetery; it was not far from the nursing home. She went there on her way back home.

Once inside the gate, it took her almost 40 minutes to find his grave. Then she saw it. It was just a simple stone, with a small cross and a small star of David on it. They had even put the star of David on his right side, she noticed, remembering his joke. The inscription read, "Herr Matthew Morgenstern." As she lay the Easter lily on his grave, she wondered what had happened to his Bible.

She stood and looked down at his resting place, then said, "Thanks, Mr. Morgenstern. Thanks very much for taking time for me."

And as she turned to leave, she thought she heard him say, "You come again sometime. *Ja?*"

"Let us not become weary in doing good, for at the proper time we will reap a harvest if we do not give up. Therefore, as we have opportunity, let us do good to all people."

Galatians 6:9-10a

Higher, Higher

If Rick had had the slightest inkling as to what would happen when he got there, he would never have gone over to the Morris's. Tom Morris was a friend of his. He had the seat right next to Rick in math, and they were both on the track team.

Rick wondered sometimes why Tom seemed to have so many friends. He had a few himself, but not as many as Tom Morris seemed to have. Maybe it was just Tom's personality. Or maybe he worked harder at it than Rick did, remembering the names of people that he met and making them feel just a little special when he talked to them. That was how Tom treated Rick, at least.

Rick had been to Tom's house frequently. Tom always had the latest records, and he had a set of body-building magazines Rick liked to look at. Rick would turn the pages, trying to imagine he was built like "Mr. Muscular America" and thinking how he could impress Sue Crawford with a build like that.

This afternoon, while they were showering after track, Tom had invited him to come over after school. Rick knew his folks would not complain; it was Friday and he had the weekend to do chores and homework. So he had gone straight home with Tom when school was out.

But now he wasn't sure exactly *what* he thought of Tom. They'd been relaxing on the carpet in Tom's room for over 40 minutes, the record player spinning, Tom's magazines spread out around them on the floor. They'd started talking about what the lyrics meant in some of the most popular hit tunes. Tom had the number three tune of the week positioned on the record player and was setting on the needle when he said, "This has to be the greatest song that's ever been recorded."

"Think so?" Rick asked, showing in his voice he wasn't quite convinced. He knew a hundred other songs he liked as well.

"Sure I do," said Tom. "Just *listen* to it." The familiar rhythm filled the room as drums and violins—and then the sudden jolt of an electric guitar—introduced the vocalist. Tom closed his eyes and started writhing with the music. "Higher, higher —Don't you know you give me fire!"

Rick liked the music well enough. He had no doubt, in fact, that it would soon be number one on all the charts. But Tom seemed really hooked on it. Rick wondered what there was about it that made Tom react that way.

"You ever think about that song?" Tom asked when it was finished.

Rick shrugged. "Not really. Just like all the rest of them, I guess. It's just a song."

"No *way*!" said Tom, starting the record again. "It's more than just *a* song. It's *the* song. Listen to that beat!" He closed his eyes again. Rick felt the drums set up a rhythm in his stomach. It made him feel like he was in a jungle. Something in him really liked the feeling. Still, another part of him felt nervous and uncomfortable about the way the music affected him. He couldn't put his finger on what bothered him about it.

The record finished for a second time.

"That guy's a genius," Tom said, taking off the record and sliding it into its cardboard sleeve. "I'll bet he makes millions a year with songs like that."

"Yeah, probably," said Rick, trying to imagine what he'd do with a million dollars.

Tom stretched out on the carpet, leaned on one side, and propped his head on his elbow and his palm. He looked at Rick with animated eyes. "You ever think about the words?"

"What? 'Higher, higher'?"

"Yeah. And: 'Now you've got control of me—deep into the soul of me—don't you know you give me fire!' Think about it."

Rick thought about it. "He's just feeling good, that's all."

Tom grinned at him. "Think so?"

"Sure. He likes the way he feels."

"But what about the *words*. 'You've got *control* of me.' That's not just feeling good, man."

"Well, it's probably a love song. They're all love songs. It's probably some girl he's thinking of."

Tom looked at him, not saying anything.

"I take it you don't think so," Rick said, shifting his position.

Tom shook his head, still grinning slightly. "Nope. I think there's more to it than that."

"So? So what *does* it mean then?"

"Just think about it."

Rick didn't get it. Tom was always doing stuff like this to him. He wouldn't tell you what he thought until you practically dragged it out of him.

"I don't know," Rick said, acting bored.

"Suppose you didn't have a girl. How else could you get high?" Tom prodded.

Drugs? Could that be what Tom meant? Rick had heard some teacher saying, in a class he'd had last year, that lots of rock songs had a hidden, drug-related meaning. But he hadn't thought too much about it.

Tom was getting up now. Rick stayed where he was. He picked up "Higher, Higher" and carelessly examined it. Tom was opening a dresser drawer and digging for something beneath the socks and underwear.

"You think he's talking about drugs?" asked Rick.

"I'm sure of it," said Tom, closing the drawer and coming back. He sat down Indian-fashion and began to spread out several items on the carpet just in front of him. Rick's eyes grew wide. Tom had the paraphernalia he'd learned to recognize from seeing the films they'd shown so many times at school.

"You ever snorted coke?" asked Tom.

"No. Never. You?"

Tom nodded. "Let me tell you, everything that music says is true."

Rick felt his blood turn cold. Tom was one of his best friends. And Tom—

"Want to?" Tom asked, almost whispering.

Rick couldn't think. His head was spinning. Tom Morris, star of the track team, everybody's pal, a whiz at math, was—

"Listen, Rick. Don't be alarmed. A lot of kids are doing it. The first time I was asked to try it, I reacted just like

66

you. It scared the devil out of me. But honestly, there's nothing like it. Nothing! You just can't believe the feeling."

Rick felt a tug inside. His best friend did it, and he seemed to be OK. It didn't seem to show on him, that he was doing it or anything. And, if it really felt as good as Tom was saying—

A rumble could be heard beneath them. "Yipes!" said Tom, collecting everything and stuffing it into the drawer and out of sight again. "You hear that? It's the door to the garage. My dad's home early."

"Listen," Rick said, getting up, "I gotta go."

"OK," Tom said. "Look—don't say anything, OK?"

"OK," Rick answered. He had no intention of getting his best friend in trouble. But something bothered him. He wondered if Tom really wanted him to try it too, or if he was just testing him. And, if he wanted him to try it, would he be able to say no? He wondered if he shouldn't try it, just one time. What would it feel like if he did?

Rick couldn't concentrate at school the next day. Every time he saw Tom, he got nervous. Luckily Tom didn't bring up the subject. In fact, it seemed to Rick that Tom had totally forgotten about what had happened. He talked about all sorts of things and joked around the way he always did. Never once was cocaine mentioned.

In his spare time, when he was sure nobody who might suspect anything would be around, Rick went to the school library and looked for information about drugs. He told the librarian he was doing a research project (which, he decided, was actually the truth). She helped him find all kinds of printed information he would never have been able to locate himself.

On Tuesday night, at supper, Rick's dad told about a close call he had had while driving home during rush hour. Someone had just missed him while changing lanes; whoever it was had finally ended up down in the ditch. Rick's father said, "I have a feeling he was driving under the influence of alcohol—or something. He could have killed somebody."

Rick tried to think of having supper with his father missing, killed in traffic. It sent a shiver down his spine.

"It's like I've always tried to tell you, Rick," his dad went on, "whenever you put something like that in your body, you no longer have control of what you're doing. And, when you're out of control, you're flirting with disaster."

He'd heard his dad say that a hundred times. He'd always thought he'd said it just to scare him. But the incident his dad had just described helped him realize that it was serious—even deadly—business.

On Thursday afternoon, in math class, Tom said, "Hey, Rick, want to come on over after school tomorrow? We can play some records and look at magazines."

"Ah—OK. Sure. I guess."

Rick tried to concentrate on math, but all he could think of was tomorrow afternoon and what Tom probably would try to get him to do.

That night at home, while he was studying for the exam in math the next day, Rick thought about Tom's invitation. Should he go? If he did, and if Tom asked him to try coke, should he give it a try?

Was it true that lots of people used cocaine and never had a problem with it? Could it get you started on the road to something worse? Would Tom be mad at him if he said no? Was it as good as Tom had said it was? He might not ever get another chance to try it. How would he know what he was missing if he didn't do it once?

He really was confused.

Rick heard his sister, Kit, get up and go into the bathroom. Why was she up in the middle of the night? He checked his watch. He'd overslept! He should be up and dressed and eating breakfast by this time.

He raced to get his clothes on. Kit had locked the bathroom door. He usually got there before her so he didn't have to wait, but this time she had beaten him. Fourth graders! They could be so slow, especially when you needed them to hurry.

Rick paced back and forth in front of the bathroom door. "You almost finished, Kit?"

"No. I need more time." Her voice came muffled through the door.

Rats. She'd make him late for sure. He poked his head inside her door. She hadn't made her bed yet. On her desk lay the spiral notebook in which she did assignments. What was this one? Some dumb poem about summer. On another page he noticed something written out in pencil. It was a creative writing exercise or something: "The Person I Admire."

He scanned the paragraph. ". . . He sometimes makes me mad, and doesn't let me use the bathroom first, and sometimes he makes fun of me. But he is honest, and he wouldn't do something to hurt you. Even though he sometimes loses his temper, he will always end up doing what is right. That's why he's the person I admire."

"I didn't say you could come in, you know." Her voice stabbed through him like a knife.

He turned and saw his sister staring at him from the doorway. He felt sheepish. "Sorry. I was waiting for the bathroom."

"Well, it's free now. Can I have my room back?"

He could tell she was irritated, but something made him ask her, "Who's this paragraph about, Kit?"

"Paragraph?"

"Right here. 'The Person I Admire.' "

"You've been snooping in my homework!"

"Just checking on your writing style. It's not too bad. But who's the person you admire?"

"If you must know—you snoop—it's you. That should be obvious, the way you hog the bathroom." She almost grinned at him. Suddenly Rick realized he hadn't used the bathroom yet and he was getting later by the minute.

He thought about his sister's essay on the way to school. In spite of the insulting parts, it really flattered him. One sentence hammered in his brain: "He will always end up doing what is right."

Before he even saw Tom coming, he had made up his mind, and he knew what he would do.

"Don't you know that you yourselves are God's temple and that God's Spirit lives in you? If anyone destroys God's temple, God will destroy him; for God's temple is sacred and you are that temple."

1 Corinthians 3:16-17

Four Minus One

Betsy Myers had to stop and catch her breath. "You kids are getting lazy. Now start pumping for a while," she said, finding a bench where she could sit down and relax.

"Push, Betsy!" Peter Sand wailed from the farthest swing.

"Nope! Can't! I'm all worn out!" she shouted at him.

This was Betsy's third year working for the city parks department. The first summer she had volunteered her services. Things had worked out so well they had hired her as a playground aide last summer, with a salary! Jon Lander, the supervisor, had been so impressed with her he'd made her supervisor of the aides this summer. She had even gotten to select the people who would be working under her.

She craned her neck to see where Kris and Stephanie were managing a softball game down at the far end of the park. Jolene was at the opposite end, helping a half dozen elementary kids weave lanyards.

"Bets!"

It was Jon's voice. She dragged herself up from the bench and headed for the recreation house. It was time

for "supervisors' huddle." Every morning she and Jon would evaluate how things were going and chart out a plan to help the aides keep busy for another day.

Jon leaned against the door frame of the building as she came toward him. Didn't he own anything but cutoff blue jeans with frayed edges? He looked good in them, though. She envied his brown arms and legs. She knew he doubled as a lifeguard, trying to collect some cash to finish college in the fall. Her income was going into savings for her own stretch at the university some day. Well, most of it. She had to have a record now and then. And Cokes and pizzas. But she saved well over half of every paycheck.

"Comin', Chief!" she said, an impudent grin on her face. She stepped inside and sat down beside Jon's cluttered desk. He sprawled out in his rickety captain's chair and propped up his feet.

"We've got Olympics for this afternoon, right?"

"Right. I think we're going to have a good turnout for that. The aides have really talked it up. I think practically everybody who's enrolled in anything is coming."

"Good. Need help with anything?"

"Nope. Just come down and cheer. They've really got it organized."

"They've worked out pretty well, haven't they?"

Betsy colored. All three of her trainees were doing outstanding work. And, only one month into summer, they had melded into a real team. Should she take the credit for it? "Yeah. They have. They've worked out really well."

Jon folded his arms behind his head and stared at the ceiling. He took a deep breath. "Bets?"

"Yes?"

Jon did not go on. He just turned his head and stared at her, frowning.

"What's the matter?"

"We've got problems."

"What kind?"

"Money."

That was nothing new. The city always seemed to be behind with revenues. Especially now, with the economy down, people out of work, and companies less profitable, all kinds of programs were beginning to be cut.

"We've got to let somebody go, Bets."

It was like a knife slicing into her. "You mean—one of the aides? Jon, we only hired them a month ago! They're counting on a job all summer!"

Jon exhaled heavily. "I know. It's rotten. But I don't know what to do."

She scowled at him. "I should have known it was too good to last. Just when the staff begins to work together, something like this happens." She trailed her canvas shoe across the floor, drawing an invisible half-moon with the toe.

"I hate this more than you do, Bets. Believe me. I've put off explaining it to you a week or more. But I just have to do something about it."

"How long have we got?"

"Till Friday."

"Friday! Jon, it's Tuesday now! That only leaves three days!"

"I know." He scratched his ear and scowled at the ceiling again. "I know. It's tough."

"So—what do we do now?"

"I'd like to ask a favor of you, Bets."

She knew what he was going to say. Her blood began to freeze.

"I wish you'd choose which one."

"You mean—I've got to fire somebody? *You're* the supervisor!"

"Yes, but you're the supervisor of the aides. You hired them. You keep better tabs on them than I do. Honestly, you have a better feel for how they work—or how they don't work. You should really be the one."

She realized he had his mind made up.

"It goes with leadership, Bets. When I made you supervisor, I gave you more responsibility. This is a part of that."

"OK," she said, her voice heavy with resignation. "But let me do it my way, OK?"

"What does that mean?"

"Let's not ruin the Olympics for them. Can I put it off until tomorrow?"

"Sure, if that's the way you want it."

The way *she* wanted it! The way she wanted it was not to fire *anybody*! But she knew that choice was not included. As she got up to go out, she felt a little dizzy. Heading down the hill toward the swings again, she wondered if she'd heard Jon right. Could she have dreamed this conversation?

As she alternated pushing kids in swings, her body doing it mechanically, she wondered how she would tell the aides, all three of them good friends of hers. And how would she decide which one to cut?

"Dad?" Betsy said, looking up from the doodling she had done on the corner of the paper she had clipped to the board on her lap.

"Hmmm?" He was still buried in the sports section.

"Dad, can I ask you a question?"

"Hmmm? Sure. What is it?" He began to turn another page, still studying the newspaper.

"Father!"

That was all it took. She never called him that unless all else had failed. He closed the paper and looked up. "OK. What is it?"

"Can I ask you something—personal?"

"Depends. What is it?"

"Last year—at your office—when they let you go—"

He shifted in his chair. She thought she saw him wince.

"Did you—you know—have anything to say about it?"

He breathed in and let it out with care. "Well—yes—and no. They asked me to react to the idea—but I knew they had their minds made up. They had to cut some-body. I turned out to be the one."

"Are you still bitter?"

"I'm not thrilled about it, if that's what you mean. But I'm lucky to have found the other job. We aren't starving. Things could be much worse."

"Dad, I've got to fire somebody at the park. I just don't know how to do it. I'm scared to death."

"That's a pretty heavy burden for somebody your age, Bets. Why can't Jon do it?"

"Well—we talked about it. And I think he's right. I hired them. I should be the one, but—"

"But?"

"I don't want to fire *any* of them. All of them are good."

"Which one of them would be hurt the least if she were cut?"

She thought about it. "You know, that's a point. Maybe one of them could handle it better than the others. If I could just—Sure! That's what I'll do! Thanks, dad!"

As she hurried from the room, her father shrugged, then turned to find what page he'd been on last.

It had been the hardest thing she'd ever done, but Betsy had at least moved some of the responsibility from her own shoulders. As she sat behind Jon's desk now, watching "her" three aides around the table in the center of the room write rapidly, their heads bent over as they concentrated on their work, she still felt heavy gloom. Why hadn't they reacted to her when she'd given them the news? What thoughts were going through their heads right now, as they attempted to defend their right to keep their jobs?

She'd given each of them a sheet of paper, a pencil, and an envelope. She'd told them to write out the reasons why they thought they should—or shouldn't—stay. She realized that one of them was going to fire herself—by arguing her case less skillfully. Or, possibly, by being generous and not fighting it, so that the other two would not be cut.

Betsy wondered if this was the way to do it. But she didn't know a better one. So she sat. And waited. And listened to the pencils scratch across their papers.

As they filed out, one by one, they handed her the envelopes in which they'd sealed their documents. She thanked each of them quietly. She thought she saw a tear in Jolene's eye when she went out. The other two were guarded, almost stern, attempting not to show emotion.

The three envelopes felt heavy in her hand as she trudged home with them. Today was Wednesday. In the morning she would have to tell the bad news to the loser, and the very next day she would have to let her go!

Betsy couldn't open the envelopes when she got home. She left them on her bed and went out to the living room to watch the evening news. Her father looked at her suspiciously. She'd never watched the evening news before.

At supper she was silent. Her mother looked uncomfortably in her direction, but she didn't force her to make conversation.

It was nine o'clock before she sat down on her bed and read what they had written. To her horror it was not at all as easy as she'd hoped. In fact, all three sounded alike. They all said things like, "I just love these kids— I've tried so hard to find a job; where would I find another one?—We're such a good team now, it really is a shame to break it up—"

She couldn't sleep. She went downstairs at 3:00 A.M. and went out on the screen porch. There she sat, in her pajamas, listening to crickets chirp and watching the moon turn shingles silver on the rooftops of the houses down the street.

She wondered if God knew how she was wrestling with her problem. She had asked him for some help two nights ago. But if God had answered, she was not sure what he'd said.

When she came in to breakfast, after having slept three hours, Betsy felt as though she hadn't slept at all.

"Oh, Bets, you have big circles underneath your eyes," her mother said. Betsy didn't answer.

"Well, have you decided what to do?"

"What would you do, mom?"

78

"Does that mean you haven't made up your mind then?"

"Betsy! Push!" wailed Peter Sand.

"Just once more," Betsy said, giving him a generous shove. "Now pump! I know you can. I've seen you do it!"

Peter started pumping. Betsy laughed inside. That little minx, she thought.

"Bets!"

Jon's voice. Time for supervisors' huddle. She felt queasy. When she was inside and sitting down, she said, "I didn't sleep all night. So no smart cracks about the way I look."

Jon eyed her cautiously. "You choose somebody to let go?"

She nodded.

"Want to tell me?"

Betsy looked him in the eye. "I'm going to fire myself."

His jaw dropped open. "What!"

"I have to, Jon. It isn't fair to any of the others any other way."

"But—you—!"

"I'll stay on as a volunteer. OK?"

"Bets, you're the most important of the four. I can't pay them and have you work for nothing."

"I was salaried last year. Give them a chance."

He looked at her in disbelief as she got up and quietly went out. Down the hill she heard young Peter Sand yell at her, "Betsy! I ran out of gas! Come push me!"

"Coming, Peter!" she yelled back, and headed in his direction.

"Do nothing out of selfish ambition or vain conceit, but in humility consider others better than yourselves. Each of you should look not only to your own interests, but also to the interests of others."

Philippians 2:3-4

Running on Empty

Carol crouched behind the speedboat, tugging tentatively on the tether. Snugging her toes into the footstrap on the ski, she looked at Kevin, at the wheel, and shouted, "Go!"

The speedboat lunged ahead, and Carol came out of the water, suddenly riding it, navigating expertly across the boat's wake. Skillfully she directed the long ski beneath her well off to the left side.

There was nothing quite like waterskiing, and she was really good at it. Kevin kept one hand on the wheel as he looked back with admiration, watching her maneuver gracefully behind. The boat began to arc majestically, leaving a great half-moon of roiling water in its path as they swept grandly through the bay.

Twelve minutes later they were back, and Carol sank into the water by the dock, exhausted and exhilarated.

Stretching out on the dock, she absorbed the welcome sun, waiting for Kevin to secure the boat. He was a couple of years ahead of her in school. She had met him when his sister, Fran, her locker-mate in gym, had brought her home and introduced them. She'd fallen for him, but she wondered if he realized it. She had never

come right out and said, "I like you, Kevin," but she really did.

She felt the dock shake as he came along it. In his usual playful way he shook the water from his hands, just recently trailed in the lake for this moment, on her warm, relaxing body. It sent shivers through her.

"Kevin! Cut it out!"

"Come on. You like it. Quit pretending otherwise."

She liked whatever Kevin did. She only wished that he liked her. Or would admit it.

He stretched out next to her, still dripping water on her. Carol drew her breath, looked sideways at him, and then, quick as lightning, shoved him off the dock into three feet of water. Scrambling up, she made it to the beach just seconds before Kevin sent a spray of water splashing up in her direction.

After he had caught up to her, wrestled her to the grass, and forced her to apologize, he sat down next to her and said what he said every time he took her out. "You're something else on skis."

She loved it: skiing—and his compliments.

"You hear about the tragedy last night?"

"No. What?"

"Shermans, down the lake a ways, lost Skip."

"That friend of yours?" Skip was 17 or so, someone Kevin had known for a year or two.

"He died right out here on the lake, while waterskiing."

"Honestly? That's horrible."

"They're trying to decide if he had heart failure or what. He was a super skier. He just let go of the rope and sank down in the water. When they got back to him, they found him floating there, not breathing. It's really weird."

What a terrible thing to happen to somebody with his whole life still in front of him! Carol had a hard time getting used to it. What if something like that would happen to Fran or Kevin or herself—?"

"Will you be ready to go back to town in, say, an hour?" Kevin asked, interrupting her thoughts.

"Huh? Oh, sure. Will your dad be ready then?"

"Nope. My dad's not going. He's decided to stay here with mom and Fran. I'll take you."

Carol's heartbeat quickened. This was too good to be true! A round trip into town and back with Kevin—just the two of them together.

Carol had been cursing her bad luck all weekend, knowing that she'd have to go back into town tonight. Her parents had insisted, though, that if she spent the weekend at Fran's family's cabin on the lake, she'd have to come back in for church on Sunday morning. It seemed like a waste of time and gasoline to her, but that was what the deal had been. Now at least she'd get a ride with Kevin into town and back with him tomorrow after church.

Sometimes she felt like a real misfit at the lake. She couldn't think of anybody here who went to church. Kevin's family didn't. He would probably sleep in tomorrow morning and then pick her up on his way out of town again. She wondered if he thought she was a little strange, attending church on weekends when almost the whole crowd of her friends were skiing, sailing, or just sleeping in.

Sometimes she wondered why she went to church at all.

"I guess the Shermans have a problem," Kevin said, as they drove into town. For once she was glad it was 40 miles one way.

"What sort of problem?"

"Skipper's funeral could be sort of awkward. They don't have a minister or anything."

"What would your family do if something happened, Kevin?"

Kevin shrugged. "Good point." He seemed to think it over as he concentrated on the road ahead. "I guess we'd have to punt." His answer didn't sound convincing.

"By the way," he said, "remind me if I don't remember first, we need to get some gas sometime before we get back to the lake. I'd hate to have to make you push."

"Are you kidding? *You* could push. I'd *steer!*" she answered, grinning impishly.

He dropped her off at her front door and took off for his own house on the other side of town. She watched him disappear from view, then trudged across the lawn. In some ways it seemed stupid to be home just now. But she resolved not to get into it with her folks again. They might just say no the next time she was asked out to the lake.

She had some trouble getting to sleep that night. The thought of Kevin's friend's young body, lying still and cold down at the funeral home, was in her mind. What must it have been like, she wondered, to be so alive one minute and then, suddenly, to be plunged into nothingness?

Pastor Samuelson had called the little kids up to the front. As they gathered around the pastor on the carpeting, Carol noticed for the first time that the windows in the worship area all had black plastic taped across them. Suddenly the lights went out. It really seemed like midnight for a minute. She could hear the kids squeal with surprise. The pastor said, "Don't worry, kids, I've got a flashlight here. Somebody turn it on for us."

But nothing happened.

"Oh, I know the problem," said the pastor. "We need a new battery. Here, try this one." They must have had a tough time doing all that in the dark, thought Carol, wondering if the second battery was any better than the first. Then a beam of light shot up into the rafters. Kids gave out with happy gasps and some of them applauded.

Pastor Samuelson said something about the fact that Jesus was the light of the world and thanked the kids for coming up. The lights came on. The pastor went into the pulpit.

"You never can be sure," he started, "when you'll end up in the dark." Carol thought of Kevin's friend. And of his parents. Then she thought of Kevin. And of Fran. And of their folks. And Kevin's comment in the car last night.

She must have missed most of the sermon, because what she next heard Pastor Samuelson say was, "Someone once said that the church is like a 'service station for sinful souls seeking salvation.' Well, if you will think back to the children's story we just had, I wonder if we couldn't say the church is somewhere you can come to get your batteries recharged. And, if we are to be lights in the darkness of this world, we really need something like that, don't we? Amen."

When she came out of church, Carol saw Kevin waiting by the curb. It seemed a little bit embarrassing. At least he could have parked around the corner where it wasn't quite so obvious. When she climbed in he said, "I've come to rescue you from this dark prison." It was clearly meant to be a joke, but suddenly it didn't seem very funny to her.

"I had a hard time sleeping," Carol said, after they'd driven for a while.

"No kidding? Why?"

"That friend of yours."

"Skip Stewart? Yeah. That's really tough."

Was that all he thought about it? "Don't you have to wonder—you know—what's become of him?"

"Of Skip? Not really. He's just gone, that's all. It's just a shame he went so soon."

"What do you mean 'just gone'?"

"I mean, it's over. When you're dead, you're dead. That's all there is, you know."

"I can't believe you really think that, Kevin."

"Well, my folks do. Anyway, that's what they say. Besides, there's nothing we can do about it. When your number's up, it's up."

She doubted that was true. After all, if someone tried to kill himself, for instance, did that mean that his "number was up"? She didn't feel like arguing with Kevin though.

"Oh, look, we're coming to a filling station. Don't you need to get some gas?"

"Yeah. But not at that one. Look. It's out of business."

"Guess you're right. I wonder why they closed it."

"Simple. People just stopped going there. Didn't take too long and they were forced to close it up."

Carol thought about it. Churches were a little like that too. What would happen if the members all reacted like she had about this weekend? No one would have come to worship. And no "batteries" would have been re-charged, to put it in the language of that story Pastor Samuelson had told.

"I guess I fooled around a little bit too long when I got home last night," said Kevin, looking at his gas gauge. "I was going to fill it, but I just let time slip by until everything was closed. This morning I slept kind of late and didn't want to keep you waiting. Now here we are, running on empty."

The church is like a service station—

Down the road another filling station could be seen, but Kevin didn't even slow for it. When they were next to it, Carol saw why. A prominent red sign said "Closed on Sundays." Now she started wondering if they would make the 40 miles back to the lake.

They finally found a place that wasn't closed. They rolled in with the gauge somewhere below the empty mark. When Kevin had turned off the key, he grinned and said, "I've never run this tank so empty in my life."

By the time they got back to the lake, Carol had made a decision. "Do you suppose we could drive down the shore a minute and stop to see the Shermans?"

"Skip's folks? Probably. But—I don't think you even know them, do you?"

"No. But—well, I'd like to extend my sympathy. They are still at their cabin, aren't they?"

"Let's see—yeah, I think they're closing it today. We'd still catch them if we went now."

As they headed for the Sherman's cabin, Carol wondered if she could convince them to consider asking Pastor Samuelson to have the funeral for their son. She'd tell them they could mention she had been the one to give them the idea. Pastor Samuelson seemed like the sort of person who would want to help them. At least, it couldn't hurt to try.

"Listen, Kevin," Carol said as they got out of the car. "I really do appreciate you and your family having me again this weekend."

"Glad to. Kind of boring with no company."

"And, Kevin—"

"Yeah?"

"In spite of the fact we almost ran out of gas, thanks for taking me into town last night. It really meant a lot to me."

More, in fact, than Kevin had the slightest inkling of.

"Do not conform any longer to the pattern of this world, but be transformed by the renewing of your mind. Then you will be able to test and approve what God's will is—his good, pleasing and perfect will."

Romans 12:2

The David's Cave Discovery

"It's who you know that counts." That's what Rick Stevens' friends had always said. Rick hadn't ever really known why they had said that—until he had tried to get a summer job. And tried. And tried.

The only reason he had gotten any job at all was that his dad had been a friend of Mr. Wilson's. Mr. Wilson had been looking for a summer fill-in person at the theatre. Rick's dad had just happened to be talking to him at the Lion's Club one noontime when the subject had come up.

And what a summer job it had turned out to be! Rick used to have to beg his folks to let him go to movies. Now the theatre paid *him* to come. Of course, he had to do some work. He ran the two projectors every night and kept a close eye on the rest of the equipment. But that left quite a bit of time to sit and watch the movie.

Rick's dad had laid down a few conditions when he'd gotten the job. If the movie wasn't fit for someone his age to be watching, Mr. Wilson had to find somebody else to work those nights. But that had not been very often. Besides, with Mr. Wilson owning two theatres, it was easy to have Rick change places with the other projectionist. Rick hadn't missed an evening's work all summer.

Rick soon had learned that things are not all glamour in the movie business. After you have seen a movie five times running, there's not much surprise left to the ending. It was worse than watching reruns on TV. When you watched a movie over and over, you got a little sick of it.

But Rick was not complaining. Some of his best friends could not get summer jobs. And, since he'd started at the theatre, his friends would call him up and ask him if the movie was worth going to. He felt important, almost like a professional film critic.

Rick had seldom taken any of the films they'd shown at the theatre too seriously. That is, until *David's Cave* had come to town. That's what all his friends were calling it. "Hey, have you seen *David's Cave*?" they'd say to one another. Or: "I thought *David's Cave* was really stupid. But I'm glad I saw it."

Actually, the film was called *The David's Cave Discovery*. The first night it had run, Rick hadn't thought a lot about it. In fact, he had had some extra errands in the projection room while the reels were playing out, so he hadn't really caught the story. But after all the phone calls afterwards, he told himself he'd better watch more carefully the second night.

It seemed that members of several churches in the city had turned out to see the film the first night—and had been alarmed at what they'd seen. It wasn't that it was a violent or a pornographic movie. It was rated G! But people who had seen it, and were phoning in, were saying it was making fun of God and Christianity—even that it could destroy your faith!

So Rick watched carefully the second night the movie ran. It was the story of a manuscript a shepherd found in some forgotten cave south of Jerusalem, supposedly a cave where David had once hidden from the half-insane King Saul. The scroll was, so the story went, a long-lost document written by eyewitnesses of Jesus' ministry. Supposedly these people had heard Jesus say that he was not the Son of God and that he was afraid people were getting the wrong idea about him. After the crucifixion, so the story went, the disciples started telling people Jesus was alive again—because they wanted to believe it. Then the action switched back to the scroll and its discovery just a year or two ago. All kinds of people tried to get it, some because they thought it would be valuable, and some because they feared it would destroy a lot of people's faith in God.

Rick noticed that a message on the screen, both at the beginning and at the end of the film, explained that this was only fiction, based upon a novel, and that as far as anybody knew there wasn't any document such as the film described.

Rick was interested in the film but not upset by it. When they were closing up that night he said to Mr. Wilson, "What do you think of the movie?"

"Me? Pure fiction. Interesting. That's all." He shrugged while he was saying it.

"You think we'll get more phone calls?"

"Yes. Probably."

"What do you say to people when they phone about it?"

"Very simple. It's a story. Make-believe. It says so two times on the screen. People are just taking it too seriously. It's just made up. It didn't happen."

Rick considered Mr. Wilson's comments after he got home. It was, of course, as he had said. It wasn't real. Nobody really did discover such a document. But, on the other hand, those people who had phoned in had a point. It could make someone doubt his or her faith. Of course, they didn't have to go and see the movie. But, if it was an attack on something that they treasured, how could they *not* go and see it, at least to get themselves informed about it!

On the third night Rick found himself watching the film with more care. He noticed things this time he'd missed before, and something started troubling him. The story actually began to sound convincing. The night before he'd sort of shrugged it off. This time it seemed more compelling to him.

That bothered him a little.

The next night when he got to work, some people were parading right in front of the ticket window, carrying signs that said things like "This Theatre Is Showing Blasphemy" and "*The David's Cave Discovery* Is an Insult to Religion!" He felt a little awkward going in, between the demonstrators. Mr. Wilson stopped him for a minute. "Boy, I'll sure be glad when this film's out of town. I'm getting sick of all this controversy."

Rick nodded. He agreed with Mr. Wilson, but for other reasons. He'd be glad to see the movie leave because the story made him squirm. In fact, he almost dreaded seeing it again. He tried ignoring it that night while it was showing, but he couldn't. The questions that had crept into his mind last night continued gnawing at him now.

Regardless if there was a "David's cave discovery" or not, was it a possibility that Jesus didn't think he was the Son of God? Could he have died and not been raised? Could his disciples simply have invented that? Rick's grandmother had died a month ago. She died believing she would be raised to new life, the way that Jesus had been raised. But if Jesus' resurrection had been simply an invention that some people had made up, then had Rick's grandmother died believing in a lie?

Rick's dad was sitting up when he got home. "Dad, you know that movie we've been showing all this week?"

"Are you kidding? There was a report on it tonight on TV news at 10 P.M."

"Really?"

"Mostly interviews with people picketing the theatre. I guess I ought to go and see it. Could you sneak me in for free?" He winked at Rick, then chuckled.

"Dad, do you know what the movie is about?"

"Just what I've heard on TV news. I think I might have read the novel. That was quite a while ago though."

"Does it bother you? I mean, to think that Jesus maybe wasn't who we think he was?"

"I still believe what I was taught in church school, Rick. Don't you?"

"Well—yes—but—"

"But you've got some questions now. Right?"

"Well—"

"Rick, when you get to the university you'll find a lot of people who make fun of God and Christianity. You can't take them too seriously."

"Yeah. I know. But—just suppose—"

"Suppose what? That the Bible's wrong? You don't believe that, do you?"

Rick decided not to push it. He got the feeling that his dad was not able to understand very well how doubts got into him sometimes. He didn't want to hurt his dad or make him feel that he was giving up on God or anything. On the other hand, he had to talk to somebody about his questions.

The next day Rick tried once more, with his mother. She was understanding—sympathetic, even. But when he got to the issue that was really on his mind, she didn't satisfy him either.

"Mom, how can we really know what's true?"

"*Really* know?"

"You know. For sure."

"Well, I guess we just have to trust. God wants us to believe what's in the Bible."

"But—what if some of it is wrong or something?"

She looked at him a long time with a slightly furrowed brow. Was she mad at him? Or worried? Or perplexed about a way to answer him? Or what? At last she said, "Well, sometimes people are sincerely wrong. I know I have been sometimes. But we have to trust to our experience. I know God is faithful. And I trust him. When I get to heaven I expect to get the answers to the questions I can't answer now." She smiled.

Rick tried returning a smile of his own. It wasn't easy. He was still not satisfied.

He never thought the night would come when he would hate to go to the theatre, but tonight he felt that way. And this was only Friday. There was still one more night of this wretched movie.

That night, after he was home in bed, he had a nightmare. He was in the movie, with the people who were writing the document. He argued with them not to write it. They just laughed at him. He grabbed the scroll and started running. People started after him. He ran still faster, but they gained on him.

When he woke up he was soaked with perspiration.

That was it. He'd had enough. He knew he had to talk to somebody. When he'd had breakfast, Rick looked up the number for the church and dialed it. The janitor was there, but not the pastor. He gave Rick the pastor's phone number at home. Rick called and asked for an appointment.

"How about this afternoon, say, 3:00?" said Pastor Jacobsen.

"That's fine. I'll be there."

When he walked into the pastor's office, Rick felt guilty. Maybe Pastor Jacobsen was still not finished with his sermon for tomorrow. Or maybe he had other, more important things to do.

"How are you, Rick? Good to see you."

"I'm just fine, thanks," he replied. Then, thinking better of it, he said, "No, I guess I'm not." He told the pastor everything.

"You've got a lot of courage, trusting me with what you're struggling with. Many people wouldn't take a risk like that."

"What kind of risk do you mean?"

"Well, that they might be laughed at. Or that I might scold them for a lack of faith."

Sort of like his dad had started sounding, Rick decided.

"If I asked you for five dollars, would you let me have that much, say, for a week?"

"Sure, if I had it," Rick said, grinning.

"Yes. That's what I meant. Now, tell me something. Why would you be willing to trust me with your money?"

"Well—because I know you—and I know you're honest."

"How do you know that?"

"I've been around you for a while. You have a reputation for not cheating people. And you preach about it. Stuff like that."

"OK. That's what I'd hoped you'd say. In other words, experience tells you you can trust me. That's the way it is with God and us. We know that God is faithful. We've experienced it. We can trust him. We can't prove it scientifically, but we can still be sure. That's how it was with Jesus and the 12 disciples."

"Could they have been wrong?"

"They could have been. But I don't think they were. They went out and did great things for him—and even suffered and got killed for him. You don't do things like that unless you're sure."

"But what if someone found a hidden Bible book or something that said Jesus wasn't who we think he is?"

"Remember, Rick. The Bible wasn't written merely so that people would believe. Those books were written because people had strong faith already. There have always been some people ready to deny God's love or power or faithfulness. Some people don't believe that germs can make you sick. But my experience tells me otherwise. It's not proof that matters in the end. It's trust— just like your mother said. It's lending me five dollars, knowing I'll be good for it. You could turn out to have been wrong—but your experience tells you otherwise."

"That's what we learned in Bible study, isn't it?" Rick asked.

"I'm glad you said that. It just proves that all those classes weren't totally a waste of time." He laughed. Rick did the same.

He thanked the pastor for his time, then double-timed it downtown to get ready for the final showing of *The David's Cave Discovery*.

"For what I received I passed on to you as of first importance: that Christ died for our sins according to the Scriptures, that he was buried, that he was raised on the third day according to the Scriptures, and that he appeared to Peter, and then to the Twelve."

1 Corinthians 15:3-5

Reunion

When they first arrived at Forty Oaks Park, Mark West wished more than ever he had stayed at home. He had never been to a reunion and he wasn't sure he wanted to get in the habit of attending them. His dad had griped for days before they'd finally agreed to come that every one he'd been to was a bore. "All they do," he'd said, "is brag about how great their lives have been. You wonder if they're lying through their teeth. And even if they're not, who needs to listen to that bragging?"

But it was his mother's relatives, the Stellars, who were holding this one. Maybe that was why his dad was not too thrilled about it. Or was it because his dad was a mechanic, and he thought it wasn't much of a profession to compare with lawyers, clergy, or presidents of banks?

They only had the Stellar family get-together every 10 years. Last time Mark was only four. They'd left him with a sitter.

"You can't blame me, can you, Mark?" his mother asked as they locked up the car and headed for the picnic grounds. "After all, who knows where you might be 10 years from now. I've got to have one chance to show you off, you know."

As though he were a horse at an exhibit! That was one thing that was bothering Mark. Another was the fact that he didn't know any of these people. They had not kept touch these last years with his mother's side. They lived so far away. He figured it would take him all day just to find out who these people were, and who was what branch on the family tree.

But most of all he worried there would be only old people, and no kids. And nothing much to do. He really wished he hadn't come.

"Watch that volleyball!" a young voice shouted, not too far away. Mark looked up and saw it coming straight for him. He caught it on the fly. A teenager about his size came over. "Hey, we need one more. You want to join the losers? Maybe with you on our side we'll trounce those show-offs. How about it?"

Mark shrugged. It would probably beat wasting time with boring introductions to a bunch of older people he had never heard of. "Sure," he said. Then, looking at his mother, he said, "OK, Mom?"

"OK." She didn't seem to be upset or anything.

Mark fired the ball back at the teenager, then walked behind him toward the net. They looked like high schoolers, and some junior highs, he thought. About a dozen on a side. How could there be so many cousins that he'd never met?

Mark fell in place next to the server in the back row. "Seven serving twelve!" the boy next to him shouted. Wham! A towering serve dropped in behind the second row across the net.

"Our point!" He served again. The volley came and went with a ferocity that Mark hadn't experienced in his years of playing volleyball. A lot of solo, show-off stuff

102

was going on, and not much teamwork. People in the back row tried to sock it clear across the net. The front row people tried to spike it, just to prove that they could do it. People were colliding with each other, almost as though there were points for getting underneath the ball.

By the time the other side had 15 points, Mark's team had 14. Someone said you had to win by two points, so they smacked another serve. Mark's team got the serve back, quickly tied it, went ahead, then lost the serve, the lead, and then the game.

"Same teams, but let's switch sides," the kid beside Mark yelled. A few dropped out, but everybody else was ready for another go at it. The play the second time around was not much more coordinated than the first game had been. Mark's team won by three.

Somebody knew where 7-Up and Pepsi had been iced. They headed in that direction. Stretching out beneath the oak trees on the grass, the ones who had been on the team with Mark began to get acquainted. Mark found it remarkable that nobody seemed interested in learning anybody else's name. They just began to talk, as though they had homeroom together or were neighbors down the street. For all Mark knew, they lived in different countries.

"What's your dad do?" someone asked Mark.

"Works for a garage. He's a mechanic."

"Really."

What did "really" mean? "And yours?"

The boy who'd asked the question shrugged. "He writes computer programs."

"Does he like it?"

"I don't know. I guess." He drained his can. "He's hardly ever home. He makes good money, but I wonder if it's worth it."

"You think that's bad," someone else piped up. "My folks both have full-time jobs. They're pulling in a hunk of money, both of them. But all they talk about is how to spend it."

"My dad's a professor," said a girl. "If I stay home and go to college where he teaches, I can go through free. That is, if he's not laid off first."

"That likely?" asked the boy beside her.

"It's possible. The way enrollments are now, colleges are cutting down. My dad's the only faculty that's left in his department now. My mom is really worried."

"What I think I'll do is go to the Air Force Academy," another girl said.

Everybody laughed.

"You think that's funny? I'm dead serious. Girls can go, you know."

"I guess that's right," Mark said. He'd read that somewhere.

"Listen," one of the boys said, "I think Uncle Cyrus plans to come to this reunion. Dad says it would be the first time ever for Old Moneybags."

"I hear Uncle Moneybags is buying a hotel chain," someone said.

"No kidding! Didn't he own grocery stores?"

"Still does. He's just got too much money. Has to spend it somewhere. 'Course, he's generous. Dad says he gives lots of it away."

"Wonder why he never had a family."

"Are you serious? Who has time for kids when you have all those stores to manage? Anyway, he spends his spare time flying off to Europe. That's where he met Greta."

"Greta?"

"Mrs. Moneybags. I think she's Scandinavian."

"That's what I'd like to do. Get rich like Uncle Cyrus."

"Naah. Not me. I want to have some fun. Like getting paid to play pro football."

"Well, it isn't likely very many of us will succeed like Uncle Moneybags. How many others in the Stellar family hit it big?"

Mark felt uncomfortable. His dad was a mechanic. No one else here had admitted that their parents worked at anything so ordinary. Did that put him and his family at the bottom of the heap?

He drained his can and got up. Nobody paid much attention as he headed back toward his parents and the other adults. As he passed a group of men he heard one say, "I just saw 'Crooked Calvin' locking up his motorcycle."

"You mean 'Crazy Cal' is here? I guess he has thick skin to want to come to one of these."

Mark kept on walking. Had his mother ever mentioned somebody named Calvin? Not that he remembered.

Sometime after six they started serving dinner. There was way too much food. Mark filled up his plate and looked for some place to sit down. One picnic table caught his eye. A man who looked a little younger than his dad was sitting at one end. A black beard with gray streaks filled out his face. He wore blue jeans and a frayed but clean denim jacket. He seemed busy eating, so Mark looked around to see where all the teens were sitting.

"Care to join me?" said the bearded one.

"Huh? Oh, well, I don't know."

"I'd sure appreciate it."

"Well—OK." Mark sat down, feeling sort of funny about joining this strange-looking individual.

"Food's good. That's why I enjoy reunions. Just too bad the Stellars wait so long between each one." The man's voice was thick and gravelly.

Mark tried not to look at him. He fixed his eyes on his plate as he tried to separate the chicken from the roast beef and the jello from the potato salad. They just didn't make plates big enough for potluck dinners.

"What's your name?"

"Mark. Mark West."

"Mine's Cal. Glad to meetcha." He chewed off a chunk of chicken from the drumstick he was holding.

Cal? Crazy Cal? Crooked Calvin? Was that who this person was?

"You Frank West's son?"

"Uh, yeah. I am."

The stranger laid the drumstick down and wiped his fingers on his napkin. Then he stuck his hand across the picnic table. "Put it there, good buddy. Really glad to get to know you. Really am." He shook Mark's hand with such a solid grip Mark wondered if he still had all five fingers afterwards. "I just saw your dad about a half hour ago. He ever mention me to you?"

"Ah—no. I guess he never did."

"No wonder. Most folks in the Stellar family don't. Your mother—she's my cousin, see—your mother doesn't like me any better than the rest of them."

"Why is that—Cal?"

"Well, I can't blame them really. Families like to keep their reputations clean and tidy if they can. Old Cal was

106

such a disappointment, I don't think they've got too much pride in me, after all is said and done. I think they'd like to saw my branch right off the family tree. That's probably the reason I keep coming to these phony family get-togethers, just to make sure they remember I belong."

"What—is there in your past that makes you such a—disappointment?"

"Nobody has told you? My, the Stellars keep their secrets well."

"I just know people call you 'Crazy Cal.' Or—"

" 'Crooked Calvin?' Yeah, I know. Well I deserved it. Once upon a time, at least. You see, son, I once had a top-notch job, in charge of the computers for a national corporation. But I found a way to—shall we say, 'adjust the books'—I siphoned money off into my bank account. And almost got away with it."

Mark stared at him, amazed. No wonder people called him "Crooked Calvin."

"I went to prison for a while. When I got out my wife had run off with another man. And I was broke. Nobody wanted me. I couldn't get a job. I got involved with other ex-prisoners having trouble just like me. We rounded up some cash and started a halfway house for men who'd been in trouble with the law. I was so broke I couldn't afford a car. I bought a motorcycle, but it didn't run quite right. I called your dad up once. He told me to come on up to his shop. He overhauled it for me, free of charge. And several times since then he's given me free tune-ups. I never have forgotten that. Your dad's a special sort of guy, young man. He never told you what he did for me?"

"No. Never."

"It's no wonder. I doubt he ever told your mother. She'd have cussed him out for helping me. She's a stubborn Stellar, just like me."

Mark could hardly believe what he was hearing.

"Funny thing, when I was doing good with the computers, Uncle Cyrus thought I was the greatest thing around. But after I had been in prison he just cut me off. I asked him several times for money for the halfway house. He wouldn't even do the courtesy of answering my phone calls or my letters."

Generous Uncle Cyrus?

"Funny, isn't it? Your dad, who isn't even in the Stellar family, is more understanding to a Stellar who's in trouble than the whole pack of relatives combined. You imitate your dad, son. I'd be proud of him if I were you."

They talked a little longer. Mark excused himself and went to get some cake. When he came back, Cal wasn't there. He went out to the parking lot. He couldn't see a motorcycle anywhere.

As they were heading home, Mark said, "There sure are lots of kinds of people in the Stellar family, aren't there?"

"Mm-hmm," his mother said.

"Which of them is the most successful, do you think?"

His mother said, "Well, Uncle Cyrus—"

"Let's not talk about him," said his father sternly.

There was silence in the front seat. In the back seat, Mark grinned, looking out the window. Someday he would ask his dad about old "Crazy Cal." In the meantime, he would have to think some more about what he should do when he got out of school.

He knew one thing for sure. He wanted it to be an occupation that would really be a help to other people. He couldn't think of anything that would be more "successful"—or more satisfying—than a job like that.

"So from now on we regard no one from a wordly point of view. Though we once regarded Christ in this way, we do so no longer. Therefore, if anyone is in Christ, he is a new creation; the old has gone, the new has come!"

2 Corinthians 5:16-17